The Revolutionary Voyage of John Quincy Adams

Dangerous Crossing

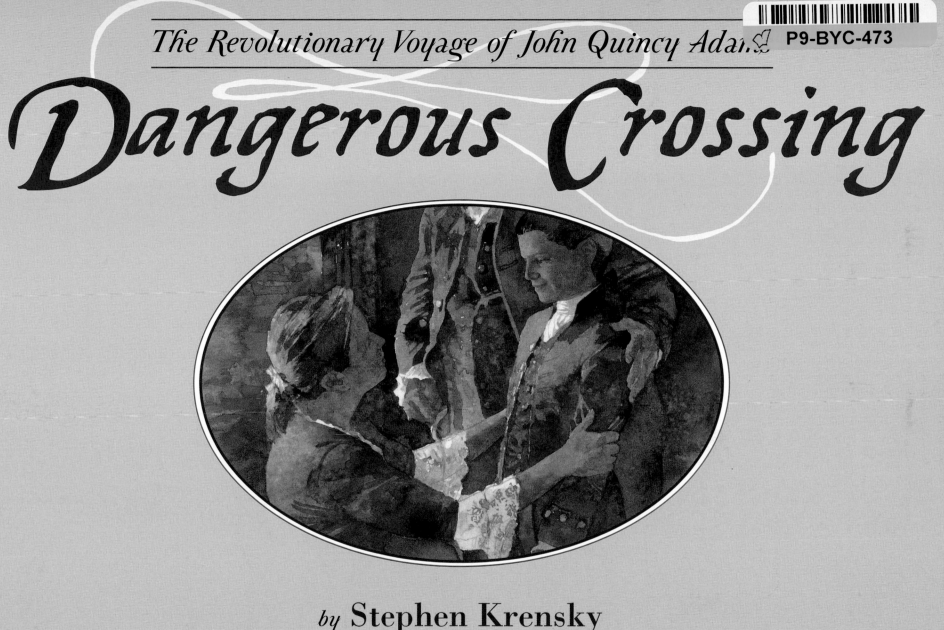

by **Stephen Krensky**

illustrated by **Greg Harlin**

DUTTON CHILDREN'S BOOKS ॐ *New York*

For Dean Morrissey, who has always been drawn to sailing ships—S.K.

For Kim—G.H.

•

Text copyright © 2005 by Stephen Krensky

Illustrations copyright © 2005 by Greg Harlin

Library of Congress Cataloging-in-Publication Data

Krensky, Stephen.

Dangerous crossing: the revolutionary voyage of John Quincy Adams /

by Stephen Krensky; illustrated by Greg Harlin.—1st ed.   p. cm.

Summary: In 1778, ten-year-old Johnny Adams and his father make a dangerous

mid-winter voyage from Massachusetts to Paris in hopes of gaining support for the

colonies during the American Revolution.

ISBN 0-525-46966-4

1. Adams, John Quincy, 1767–1848—Childhood and youth—Juvenile fiction.

2. Adams, John, 1735–1826—Juvenile fiction. 3. United States—History—Revolution,

1775–1783—Juvenile fiction. [1. Adams, John Quincy, 1767–1848—Childhood and youth.

2. Adams, John, 1735–1826—Fiction. 3. United States—History—Revolution, 1775–1783.

4. Voyages and travels—Fiction.] I. Harlin, Greg, ill. II. Title.

PZ7.K883Dan 2005   [Fic]—dc21   2003040852

Published in the United States by Dutton Children's Books,

a division of Penguin Young Readers Group

345 Hudson Street, New York, New York 10014

www.penguin.com

Manufactured in China

First Edition

1 3 5 7 9 10 8 6 4 2

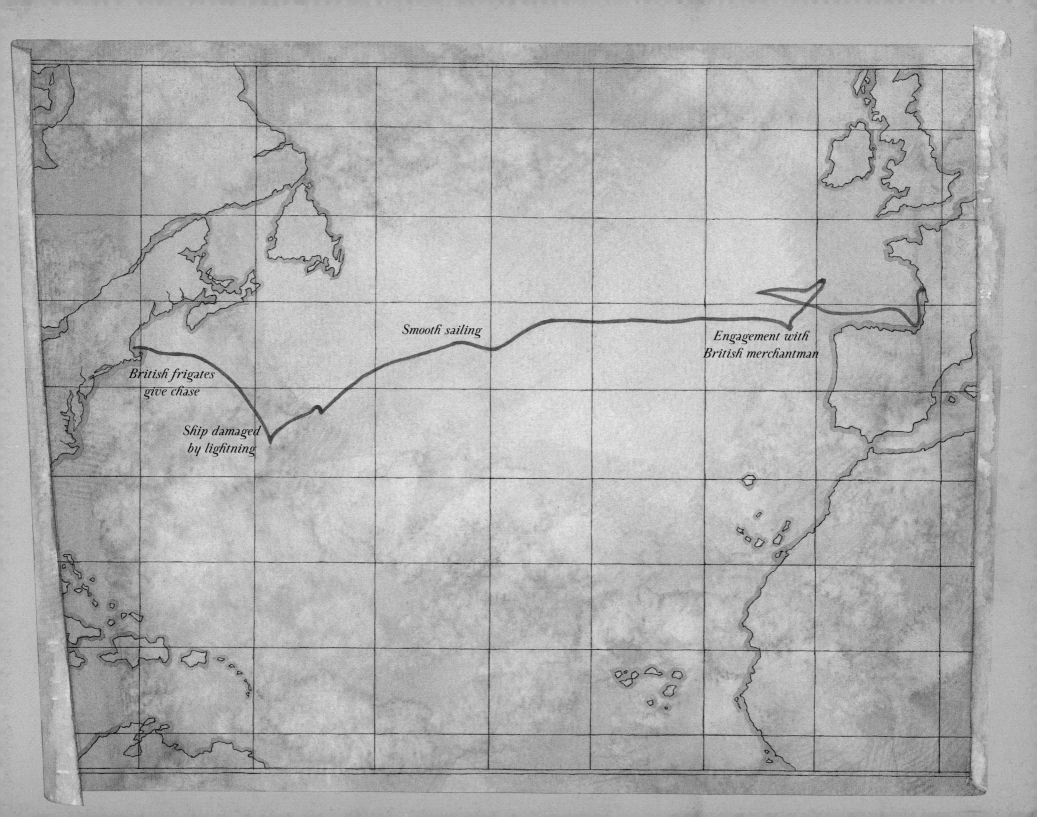

Smooth sailing

Engagement with
British merchantman

British frigates
give chase

Ship damaged
by lightning

Young Johnny Adams could hardly believe his good fortune. On a cold February day in 1778, he stood at the ocean's edge, a few miles from home. The wind blew fiercely around him, and the blustering snow stung his cheeks like nettles.

But Johnny didn't mind. Ten years old, he had never been farther than a day's ride from home. Yet here he was, about to sail to France with his father. What did stinging cheeks matter compared to that? He could still hear the words that an elderly cousin had declared in warning.

"Mr. Adams, you are going to embark under very threatening signs. The heavens frown, the clouds roll, the hollow winds howl, the waves of the sea roar upon the beach."

Johnny could not have been more pleased.

Soon the barge arrived to fetch them to the ship waiting offshore. Although they were leaving Massachusetts in a hurry and in secret, they were not going unprepared. Their baggage included two fat sheep, two hogs, one barrel of apples, five bushels of corn, some chocolate, sugar, eggs, paper, quills, ink, a double mattress, a comforter, and a pillow.

There was room for it all, and soon father and son were settled in some dry hay, bobbing up and down like corks in a bottle.

It was dangerous to cross the ocean in mid-winter, but time was pressing. The war with England, now almost three years old, was not going well. The rebel army had barely limped into their winter quarters. Many colonial soldiers lacked muskets and powder. They were also short of clothes, blankets, and shoes.

The new Americans desperately needed the support of other countries—especially France, England's greatest rival. Other representatives were in Paris already, but their progress was uncertain. It was hoped that the calm and thoughtful John Adams could do more.

Captain Samuel Tucker welcomed Johnny and his father aboard just before dusk.

Captain Tucker's new twenty-four-gun frigate, the *Boston*, had a deck more than a hundred feet long. Three towering masts stood guard overhead, clothed in endless furls of sail.

Down below, the view was less grand. The passageways were cramped, and everywhere was a terrible smell—of sea and sailors mingled together. Johnny and his father found their tiny cabin clean, at least, and with their blankets and pillows, it felt a little like home.

Once the *Boston* put out to sea, Johnny noticed a change. The waves looked bigger. They felt bigger, too. A strange feeling swept over him. His head was spinning, and his stomach as well. He soon took to his bed, glad that his groans were lost amid the creaking masts and the howling wind.

Though John Adams also felt ill, he distracted himself by writing in his diary. "Seasickness," he wrote, "*seems to be the Effect of Agitation....The Smoke of Seacoal, the Smell of stagnant putrid Water, the odour of the Ship where the Sailors sleep, or any other offensive Odor*" would not trigger it alone.

No doubt this was good to know, but it did not make Johnny feel any better.

The next day, a calmer sea improved everyone's mood. Johnny and his father returned to the deck, glad for a breath of fresh air.

"A ship on the weather quarter!" shouted the lookout.

Captain Tucker turned his glass upon the distant speck. Actually, there were three ships, and British frigates by the look of them. He was not pleased with the three-to-one odds.

But his officers protested. "We will not run from an enemy before we see him," they said. "We will not fly from danger before we know we are in it."

Besides, they were thinking, what if these were merchant ships loaded with valuable goods?

Bowing to their enthusiasm, the captain ordered the *Boston* closer.

It was soon clear, though, that his fears were well founded. These were frigates, indeed. And from their viewpoint, the odds were just right.

All three now gave chase. Two quickly fell behind, but the third kept pace. For two more days, it followed them. The sailors on watch said the frigate was closing the gap, but Johnny could not tell. His eyes were not as sharp as theirs.

"Our Powder and Balls were placed by the Guns," his father noted in his diary, *"and every thing ready to begin the Action."*

Almost three years earlier, Johnny and his mother had stood on high ground, watching the Battle of Bunker Hill eight miles away. But that had been almost make-believe, little more than flashes of light and distant cries.

Here, he would be right in the thick of things. Cannons would fire and swords flash. One of the ships would be boarded. The two crews would grapple with knives and pistols and anything else that came to hand.

An officer interrupted Johnny's thoughts. He and his father should take shelter below. As if the frigate wasn't trouble enough, a storm was coming.

They went straight to their cabin. Soon the ship began to pitch, rocking violently back and forth. They could not sit or stand without being knocked about. "It was with the utmost difficulty," John Adams remembered, "that my little son and I could hold ourselves in bed with both our hands, and bracing ourselves against the boards, planks, and timbers with our feet."

Suddenly, there was a flash of light. *C-R-R-AAACK!* The ship shuddered from the blow. Johnny and his father shared a worried glance. Was that cannon fire? Had the British frigate overtaken them? Would the firing continue until they surrendered? Or would the *Boston* fight until it sank beneath the waves?

In truth, there were no cannons at work.

"The ship has been struck by lightning!" an officer told them. The main mast was shattered, and four crew members were hurt.

For three more days and nights, the storm continued. Chests and casks were tossed about like straw, and no one could stay dry or walk steadily on deck. "The Wind blowing against the current . . . produced a tumbling Sea," Adams observed. "Vast mountains of water breaking on the ship threatened to bury us all at once in the deep."

Through it all, Johnny was proud that his father stayed calm. He was a practical man, and there was nothing to gain by making a fuss.

"Pray God protect us and carry us through our various troubles," said the captain.

Johnny and his father felt the same way.

Finally, the skies cleared. But the pale sunlight fell on a broken ship. Sails were ripped, masts splintered. Even worse, the *Boston* had been blown hundreds of miles off course. As the captain surveyed the damage, he had only one bit of good news. At least the British frigate was gone.

As the sailors began making repairs, Johnny took some French lessons from the ship's doctor and learned the names of the sails. "I am most satisfied with myself," Johnny had once told his father, "when I have applied part of my time to some useful employment."

One day a sailor pulled up a Portuguese man-of-war in a bucket. Johnny looked on in wonder. Was this truly a fish from the sea? *"Careful,"* the sailor warned him. One touch of its twisted cords would sting like a hundred bees.

Johnny's father and the captain often spoke together of their mission and the conduct of the ship. Even from a distance, Johnny recognized his father's impatience. He spoke of a ship at sea "as a kind of prison." He was especially tired of the view. "We see nothing but Sky, Clouds, and Sea," he noted. "And then Seas, Clouds, and Sky."

After four weeks at sea, the *Boston* spotted another ship—a British merchant-man loaded with precious goods. This was a prize worth catching. The passengers were ordered below as the *Boston* let out its sails.

But while Johnny and the rest stayed put, John Adams returned to the deck. He heard a loud boom—and then a cannonball shot over his head. The other ship had fired on them! Captain Tucker ordered the *Boston* brought about so that the merchantman could see the strength of her guns. Would the enemy captain, Adams wondered, choose to sink or surrender?

The surrender came quickly. The crew of the merchantman were taken prisoner, and their ship remanned with some of the *Boston*'s sailors. But even in victory, Captain Tucker was angry at Johnny's father for risking his life by returning to the deck.

"My dear sir, how came you here?" he asked. Had Adams forgotten his mission? Wasn't his safe arrival in France of the greatest importance to the Revolution?

John Adams stood his ground. "I ought to do my fair share of fighting," he explained simply. Johnny was not surprised. Until now, his father had been defending his country with ideas and words. But he would not shrink from any conflict if the cause was just.

On March 24, the *Boston* saw the coast of Europe at last, and soon they reached their port in France. "The Pleasure resulting from the Sight of Land, Cattle, Houses, &c. after so long and dangerous a voyage is very great," John Adams observed. He and Johnny had survived storms and seasickness, boredom and battles. They had seen firsthand that war was not all glory and games. They had seen men die and tested their own courage as well.

But the real adventure still lay ahead. Americans would need much help to achieve their freedom, and Johnny and his father were glad to be a part of it.

This story is drawn from John Adams's own diary, which, with an eye toward history, he kept in scrupulous detail. Adams was forty-two years old when he boarded the *Boston* in the winter of 1778. A well-established lawyer, he was a delegate to the Continental Congress and had played a role in drafting the Declaration of Independence. While in France, he worked successfully to secure French aid for the rebelling colonists. He later returned to Europe on other official missions, helped negotiate the peace treaty with England, and became the first American minister to Great Britain. In 1789 John Adams became the first vice president of the new United States and was elected as the second president in 1796. He died on July 4, 1826.

Young Johnny Adams had no idea that his trip to France was the first step toward a long and distinguished career. Over the next few years, he traveled with his father or other officials through Holland, the German states, Russia, Scandinavia, and Great Britain. In 1794, President Washington appointed twenty-six-year-old Johnny, now known by his full name, John Quincy Adams, minister to the Netherlands. He was also a U.S. senator from Massachusetts, minister to Russia, and secretary of state. In 1825 he became the sixth president of the United States. Following his one term, he was elected to Congress in 1830—the only former president ever to do that—and served until his death in 1848.